sympathetic magic

CRAB ORCHARD SERIES IN POETRY

Editor's Selection

sympathetic magic

AMY FLEURY

Crab Orchard Review &
Southern Illinois University Press
Carbondale and Edwardsville

16 15 14 13   4 3 2 1

The Crab Orchard Series in Poetry is a joint publishing
venture of Southern Illinois University Press and *Crab
Orchard Review*. This series has been made possible by
the generous support of the Office of the President of
Southern Illinois University and the Office of the Vice
Chancellor for Academic Affairs and Provost at South-
ern Illinois University Carbondale.

Crab Orchard Series in Poetry Editor: Jon Tribble

Library of Congress Cataloging-in-Publication Data
Fleury, Amy, 1970–
Sympathetic magic / Amy Fleury.
   p. cm. — (Crab Orchard series in poetry)
ISBN 978-0-8093-3224-3 (pbk. : alk. paper) — ISBN 0-8093-
3224-8 (pbk. : alk. paper) — ISBN 978-0-8093-3225-0
(ebook) — ISBN 0-8093-3225-6 (ebook)
I. Title.
PS3606.L489S96 2013
811'.6—dc23   2012036795

for Mark

Sympathetic magic . . . assume[s] that things act on each
other at a distance through a secret sympathy, the impulse
being transmitted from one to the other by means of
what we may conceive as a kind of invisible ether. . . .

~Sir James Frazer, *The Golden Bough* (1922)

And whoever walks a furlong without sympathy
walks to his own funeral drest in his shroud.
And I or you pocketless of a dime may
purchase the pick of the earth.

~Walt Whitman, from *Leaves of Grass* (1855)

Let us rather be thankful that our sorrow lives in us as an
indestructible force, only changing its form, as forces do,
and passing from pain into sympathy—the one poor word
which includes all our best insight and our best love.

~George Eliot, *Adam Bede* (1859)

Contents

Acknowledgments

Grateful acknowledgement is made to the editors of the following publications, in which these poems first appeared:

32 Poems: "Here in Topeka"
200 New Mexico Poems: "Pacheco Burn"
American Literary Review: "Sympathetic Magic"
Copper Nickel: "Elk Skeleton"
Crazyhorse: "Ablution" and "Two Solitudes"
descant: "Vigil"
Flint Hills Review: "Sky Judge" and "Hospital Time"
Flyway: "First Morel," "At the Geographic Center," "A Brief History of Barbed Wire," and "When at Last I Join"
Kansas City Star: "See You in the Funny Papers"
Kansas City Voices: "Assumptions" and "Galileo's Finger"
Measure: "The Head of St. Catherine"
Midwest Quarterly: "Home Altar"
Mikrokosmos: "At Thirty-Five" and "Magnetic Resonance"
minnesota review: "The Fort"
River Styx: "Penmanship"
seven-eight-five: "Verdure" and "Vocabulary of Ashes"
Southern Indiana Review: "In a Foreign City," "Sister Anonymous," "Specimens" and "Spiritus Mundi"

"Here in Topeka" and "Spiritus Mundi" appeared in *Begin Again: 150 Kansas Poems* (Woodley Press, 2011).

"Assumptions" appeared in *In Their Cups: Poems about Drinking Places, Drinks, and Drinkers* (Harvard Common Press, 2010).

Some of the poems in this collection were included in the chapbook *Reliquaries of the Lesser Saints* (RopeWalk Press, 2010).

Warmest thanks go to Tom Averill, Jacob Blevins, Allen Braden, Karen Chase, Neil Connelly, Robin Getzen, Jeffrey Ann Goudie, Ruth Goudie, Howard Faulkner, Keagan LeJeune, Justin Marable, Ron Mitchell, Margy Stewart, and John Wood for their generous support. I offer my deepest gratitude to my family, especially Paula and Eldon Fleury, Mark Fleury, and Derek Blakeley for their abiding love. I am also profoundly grateful to Jon Tribble, whose integrity, generosity, and dedication are an inspiration.

I especially thank the Berkshire Taconic Foundation/Amy Clampitt Fund for the gift of time and space in Amy's house, where many of these poems were written.

I.

Sympathetic Magic

The stray dog limped through traffic,
tugged by the invisible leash over miles
and years and griefs to rest her head
in your lap, trusting you with her sleep.

Sometimes what is needed comes to hand—
a book fallen open to a page of benediction,
the balm of song from the car radio's dial,
a pocket-laundered dollar to pay the toll.

In distress, you wish for an apocryphal Veronica
and she arrives at your side, offering
her only tissue, dabbing at your actual eyes.
But darkness still comes before day is yet done.

Like a dowsing rod, you lean toward
whatever is coming to you, the waters
of loving, the sump of loss. Lean in.

Elk Skeleton

Down the draw at dusk seven mule deer come
to browse the blanched grasses around the cabin.
Not all has been winter-killed this early April
as these timid sisters nudge the bitter tufts.
        Rose-gold floods their flanks.
                Soon all shadows leach away.

Come morning, frost ferns the windowpanes
and my breath disrupts moth-dust on the sill.
The branches of fog-haunted firs appear
to have been assembled from brackish ash.
        Lichen brocades the stones hove
                from this forest's decay.

At the trailhead, I find an elk skeleton,
its wind-strummed ribs like the empty staves
of a stranded, sunlit ship in the scree.
Gone the ruminant heart, the once pink
        and capacious lungs. On its spine
                a moth opens its delicate hinge.

First Morel

Up from wood rot,
wrinkling up from duff
and homely damps,
spore-born and cauled
like a meager seer,
it pushes aside earth
to make a small place
from decay. Bashful,
it brings honeycombed
news from below
of the coming plenty
and everything rising.

The Fort

When we'd grown bored of the birth-slick piglets
squirming in the farrowing house's false heat,
we left to climb the gate and gallop through pasture,
coats hung open, our hands October raw.

Crossing a fallen elm over the creek
into my uncle's timber, our pack of cousins
turned half-feral at the scent of rotting leaves,
yipping and kicking through brush up to our knees.

The fort was just past where a doe had bedded down,
the wallow a reminder of our place among things.
We'd made a shelter of sorts with what we could scrounge
from the trash ditch—sheets of tin, a rain-buckled door,
and best of all, the rusted DeKalb flying corn.

Those boys wanted a war so they went hunting
for hedge balls and walnuts and hard cow flops to hurl,
and I, the only girl, stayed behind to make do,
arranging our places around the pretend fire.

Gathering bundles of bittersweet alone,
I liked how being there made me feel wild inside.
I could squat to make a steaming circle of pee
and I could say *damn* out loud if I wanted.

At last they ran back puffing their heifer-wet breath
and dragging grubby sleeves across their noses.
From the one dented pie plate, I served a slurry
of rainwater and dirt we lifted to our mouths
with invisible spoons. When the quiet came
and the gray flannel of evening dropped
down on our haven, our hovel, the same,

it wasn't darkness or cold that moved us
toward home. Always it was hunger.

Penmanship

Opening the shoebox of my grandmother's letters
is to receive again the pillowy words she wrote
to the girl I once was. Those portly loops curlicue
across her pastel stationery—silly, yet I still love
how the sturdy girth of her Rs and her bosomy Bs
carry their prodigious pocketbooks to town
with the chubby vowels somersaulting after.
I practiced my cursive when I wrote her back,
using gray sheets from the Big Chief tablet.
At school, my teacher, whom I otherwise adored,
lassoed my letters with red ink, tried to stanchion
my hand in the lines of Palmer Method exercises.

Since then I've made a study of it, the slant
and weight of a pen stroke, this dying art—
the means by which we might come to know
one another, how we wish to be understood.
My mother's writing, pin-neat, is a steady stitch
sewn into grocery lists and valentines, ending
each line with the snipped thread of a sentence,
while my dad, who rightly prefers to type,
has a style that looks like somebody dumped out
a drawer full of forks and rubber bands,
his signature jouncing down a mile of bad road.
And the seismograph of my brother's notes
scrape the page with a series of halts and peaks.

Years of grading student essays have taught me
to decipher crimped print that embosses thought
on paper; slashes, both erratic and brash;
girlish, licorice twists; and briary marginalia.
My friend sends an inscrutable postcard from Greece,
and in the library, I squint over the great poet's words,
so trembly and faint that graphite seems to evaporate
into pure essence. My own script, fluid and elliptical,
is a visceral pleasure, given the momentum of the pen.
The last upstroke, a scarf unfurled in a gust of wind.

Bicentennial Year

Everything was at sevens and sixes
in Mrs. Slocum's class. I would turn six
four days after America's birthday.
It was the year I learned to read
and I was in love with Buck Owens.
We drew letters with circles and lines,
then sounded them out to make words.
For weeks my bottom tooth was loose.
During tornado drills we had to cover
our heads and try to keep quiet.
Grown-ups said *Nixon* like a sneeze.
Buck's guitar was blue, white, and red.
On Saturday nights at six, he picked it
and sang and sat on a hay bale.
At school we got stars for being
courteous, helpful, and neat.
After the morning bell we faced the flag
and said the pledge of allegiance.

Assumptions

Only the plain girls stay in this town
where the quiet is so violent
that sidewalks seethe and pitch,
where wind will chasten a face.

Beyond yawning gates,
the church spire punctures
pure sky and transgressions
are never forgiven.

Flags snap to tatters along Main,
and only the tavern stays open
to take in the solemn patrons,
the rich shit smell of feedlots
clinging to their dollar bills.

The register rings to the rhythm
of guest checks pierced on a spindle
and the twitch of the driftwood clock.
Red beers all around and the radio
offers the farm market report:

feeder cattle steady to a dollar higher,
soybeans rally at close of day.
And outside, what some people mistake
for empty space exalts its mute palette

while drivers pass through on their way
to Denver, Omaha, or some other
butter and egg route. Whatever you believe
about a place, well, it's going to be true.

Farm Auction

Contrails scrawl the sky under which
sawhorse-and-lumber tables offer up
the hoard and store of fifty years.
Neighbors have come to scour house
and barn and implement shed.
Yes, we've come to haul it all away—
their nests of pillows and quilts
and feather ticks, the glazed plates
and bread crocks, a washtub rimed
with bluing, the saltcellar and gravy boat,
her cross-stitch sampler and figurines,
canning jars, seals, lids. And spools
of baling wire, seed drills, spades,
coffee cans of bolts and bent nails,
a burlap-wrapped schnapps bottle
he kept back of the barn's fuse box and all
his spare fuses. An aerial photo of their farm.
And even the rusted harrow in the ditch.

The auctioneer works to disperse
all their worldly goods, singing *hey*
somebody give me twenty now, twenty
as his wife hands over odd boxes
of cribbage boards and crucifixes
to the ladies fanning themselves
with sale bills by the tilting lilacs.
From the porch the 4-H club sells
plates of peach pie and waxy cups of pop.

Inside, the smell of silage still clings
to his chambray shirt hung
on the backdoor peg after choring.
How, in stocking feet, he loved to step
on the warm place where the dog had lain,
where dilapidated hips collapsed her
in a sleeping, yellow heap.

Now all is echo where once they sat
together with the ledger, adding columns
of crop yields and prices per bushel,
or thumbing rosaries like they shelled peas—
dutiful, dutiful to the ceaseless seasons,
to their tillage and cattle and kin.
Through the window screen comes little gusts
and the sound of the gavel coming down.

II.

At the Geographic Center

of the contiguous United States,
just beyond Lebanon, Kansas,
I lie down, making my body an X
to mark the middle, the nation's navel.
Here this compass gives my bearing,
each leg and arm seeking its own
ordinal direction. Above me nothing
but the soft prospect of sky, a skiff
of cirrus clouds and no horizon.
My heart is at the heart of my country.

A Brief History of Barbed Wire

The horizon was traipsing away west
and that vast land did not know it was owned.

Acres were platted and plotted and plowed.
The fly-vexed cattle of the dominion

were herded, made to graze given pastures.
Now a deputation of starlings alights the fence,

which does not hold snowmelt, pollen or smoke,
not the hawk, not the shadow of the hawk.

Evenings the strung wire thrums a hymn of wind.

Here in Topeka

In a neighborhood of old shade, maple seeds helix down,
      winging onto windshields, mixing
with the berry-smeared shit of birds and clotting the gutters.

      From this wide porch of the Middle West,
one can hear supper plates clatter and the responsible hum
      of leafblowers. It's the dog-walking hour

when screen doors bang and the neighbor's ex drives past,
      bass strafing the place. He's just trying
to get a look at his kid on the way to his railyard shift.

      Amid the iteration of American four-squares
and airplane bungalows, the people of this town are coupled up
      and hunkering down. Here the weathervane

has rusted east, pointing toward the statehouse, where books
      first happened to young Langston Hughes,
and in Curry's famous mural, sulfurous clouds muscle above

      John Brown's fierce Bible and rifle stance,
fire flagging at his back, blood and the dead under his boots.
      When streetlamps judder on, it's time to go in

to the placid tones of the local newscaster's evening report
      on the usual city council incivilities.
The radar forecasts what the wind chimes already know.

Verdure

Something burst out that was unwanted—
the unchecked verdure of temper, a riot
of pollen and sweat. Beside prim tulips, peonies'
greening knots explode to tender shreds.
Bees hover, nuzzling cankered buds spread
open to the thrumming sun. All runs to ruin
in such a reckless garden. Trumpet vine scrolls
in vulgar abundance up the trellis. Hyacinth bean
threads the fence, mint swaths the path, and ivy
thorns through the window screen, seizes the eaves,
damning all our plans and petty designs.
Thrust up like thumbs through the soil, grubs
are routed and devoured by a fat jay.
Glory be to that which will not be contained.

Home Altar

Slatted with planks of light hewn from south-arcing sun,
     the table offers the perfume of bruised pears
and a dish of rose petals from a poet's mountain grave.
All that fractured affection lengthens along the floorboards.
     And such an upgathering of dust demands a deep
attention, invites the eyes upward. A trinity of candles burns
in steady petition to the household gods who will
     or cannot intercede on behalf of our middling,
familiar wants. Ancestors gaze out of their oval frames,
proof that what is adored can be destroyed. It does not deter
     our asking, however, and it does not diminish the urgency
of our wishing. We all live under the self-same moon,
no matter the phase. Though the tiny flames will stutter out
     and some prayers may escape from between the spaces
of our palms, never will there be an end to praying.

Vocabulary of Ashes

Tonight my mind plunges with crows
and this blood strobes its circuitry
with something prophetic, oracular,
lunatic. I want to be a sibyl.
I want words to rain down like miracle,
runneling down the trough of my arms,
rinsing the subtle light from my wrists.

What's become of my pentecostal tongue
stoking its vocabulary of ashes?
Instead, a mute augury rests in the grave
of my mouth. There is nothing left to name.
All of history is so much bone-lumber,
stacked and limed, and the future is heaped
deep and high with more of the same.

In a dark time, some men stride on pridefully
while their hearts fester in their chests.
Their forked voices abrade the airwaves
of alleyways and avenues, and we invite it.
Thunder adds its statement, answering
such improvidence with a promise
of ruin. Lightning swastikas the horizon,

and entire elegies spill from our eyes.
On what tablet is it written, on what sacred
scroll, the means by which we must atone?
I have studied the vast psalter of sky
and it has taught me nearly nothing.
Let this night's fierce angels singe the edges
of all the days to come with the fire of mercy.

At Thirty-Five

As if to prove it could serve its purpose,
her belly swelled with a tumorous womb.
The surgeon sliced it open and found
a half dozen lumpen ciphers, like a sack
of lemons or a clutch of eggs. She was delivered
of the fibrous brood, stitched up and sent back
to her life as a blood sloughing woman,
thirty-five, and mother of nothing.

Two Solitudes

I.

Awake in the bleakest part of the night,
I listen to rain fall like apology,
kneading the pillow to its fresher side.
At last I kick free from the rucked up sheets
and feel my way down the hall, through rooms
made strange by furniture sketched against
muzzy gray. There is no husband in this house
as I once thought there would be, no children
turning in easeful sleep. At the stove I twist
the knob till the thwicking burner ignites
a blue ring that breathes to bring the teapot
to a pitch pipe hum. Perhaps, all along,
I have been misreading the dark.

II.

Standing amid the understory's frostheave
and fretwork of fern, I listen to the patois
of thaw tell, in seeps and soughs, the secrets
of this ice-crazed lake. Such an afternoon
is cold enough to scour my lungs, to prick tears
from my eyes, making a prism of birch light.
All the intimacy of winter comes down
to these quiet footfalls in the snow. I gather
an armload of wood so that I might make
a little fire for myself in the evening.

III.

Sister Anonymous

They discover the dead girl
in a culvert, blood corsaging
her white fluttering blouse,
an embarrassment of bloated
limbs, broken teeth, a face
gemmed over with scabs.
Nearby ants scribble their hill,
beginning a campaign
for her last moist places.

Some say it began in a truck stop's
glass-spangled parking lot,
the hum and fog of the rigs' exhaust
muffling the shouts that followed her
this far down the state highway,
where a V of geese drags its shadow
across winter's brittle pastures.
Of course, who can know for certain?

Dear sister anonymous, dead
on the side of the road, where
is your coat? The one your mother
buttoned up to your chin,
sending you off on that errand
from which you never came home.

Niches

~

The split husk of a locust
latches to the burr oak's bark.
In the upper limbs squirrels
clack their castanets
as the reborn throb and keen
through the unevening hours.

~

The dog sniffs a fallen nest
at the sidewalk's edge.
Threaded through the twigs,
a flag, the tiny kind often seen
at graves and parades.

~

Found in a New Mexico cave,
a hunting net spun from hanks
of human hair lay four hundred years
in a pit where it was left for blessing.
The mile and a half of cordage
required sixty-nine full heads of hair,
yet its maker never returned for it.

~

The late sun cast an archipelago
of light in the campyard at Terezín.
I stooped to fill a film canister
with dirt. Tasting the dust on my tongue,
I knuckled grit from my watery eyes.

~

In the little fort by the river we kept
a cache of musty mattress batting to nestle
the fine bones of mice and rusted railroad ties
and acorn caps that we fitted on our fingertips.

~

Walking the Flint Hills with Harley,
we crouched down to find crinoids,
those chalky fossils dislodged
from their limestone seabed, gave them
to Bill, who pocketed them to bring
to his daughter to string together,
with her small, sure hands, a necklace.

~

A spider tatting a hammock in the lintel
attempts to gather light in its gauze.

~

Four days in the Holy Cross, 11,000 feet,
and we met no one. Hiking the ridge above camp
we could see down to the rock from which Elizabeth
took her yawping leap into the frigid Josephine.
Hidden in the cairn at the peak we found a jar,
a small tablet inside of it, and written on a page,
the name of a friend. The other day I read
that a small plane crashed there in the scree.

~

In the grotto where Bernadette knelt
to place her hands in the gouting wound
of the Pyrenees, to lift her eyes
to the eternal mother, the spring purls
into jugs and vials, into our cupped hands.
There is enough water for everyone
to have as much as they want.

~

At dawn of spring equinox the sun
glisters forth through the door
of the great kiva. Be it this way.

Specimens

Museé de Zoologie, Lausanne, Switzerland

Past the dusty dioramas of otters and sloths,
of roe bucks tangled in endless antler clash,
past the cases of the pinned iridescence
of Nabokov's lepidoptera, the jarred hearts
and flensed abdomens of typical human
specimens, beyond taxonomy and belief
are the glass cabinets which contain
the reliquaries of the lesser saints—
some poor mother's water-headed baby,
and one with a parasitic twin, a limbless
lifeless fetus, and a double-faced kitten,
a six-legged lamb and a cycloptic piglet—
suspended in their dreamy brine
after gathering a few breaths or none,
each having too much or not enough
of some essential thing, which is,
in the end, the source of all suffering.

Galileo's Finger

Museo di Storia della Scienza, Florence, Italy

The ecstatic canticle of his name:
Galileo Galilei, that master,
father of physics, science's martyr.
Centuries have shed false heresy's shame.
His finger points to the heavenly claim,
though enshrined in glass and alabaster,
that the sun, not the earth, is a fixed star.
Expect favor, like the phased moon, to wane
and wax again. One thin digit amid
astrolabes, sextants, armillary spheres,
exiled from his shriven corpus brought down
to Santa Croce from hills where he hid.
May his soul assume a place with seekers
and sages. Here we'll venerate his bones.

The Head of St. Catherine

Basilica di San Domenico, Siena, Italy

Among the incorruptibles this bride
of Christ offers her cowled, leather-taut face
as icon of all that's pious and chaste.
Behind a golden grate, her head, enshrined,
was once borne through Siena sanctified
and severed. Serenely it now betrays
a body scourged, scalded, and starved to grace.
Such discipline is its own kind of pride.
Her exquisite desire to suffer flared
and blazed, but the wise ones have said that faith
without works is dead. So Catherine cared
for the poor and pocked, healed schism and plague.
Through all her radiant deeds she prepared
long for the withered visage of a saint.

Ex Voto

Dear Saint Joseph, patron of husbands,
I thank you for not letting me marry
the wrong man, the one who slammed me
against doorjambs and called me a cunt.
Tonight I light a candle for that woman
I might have been had it not been for you.

~

Oh Joseph, protector of fathers,
whose aspect is a lily-flowering staff,
I am grateful my dad survived affliction
long enough to forgive my thousand faults,
no longer remembersome of my back talk
nor of his own silent disaffection.

~

The mallet and miter are the tools
of your honorable work, Joseph.
You've guided my hands in dishwater and dirt,
at factories, in nurseries, and on the page.
Please, Joseph, I have this last favor to ask,
that I might make something sturdy and true.

See You in the Funny Papers

The dog's breath hangs like a frosty conversation balloon
in a cartoon about a woman and her dog who go for a walk
on New Year's Eve. This particular woman (a single gal,
of course) wears sweat pants, flannel coat, and a stocking cap
pulled over her ears. She wonders what the dog might say
if the dog could talk (because often dogs can and do talk
in comic strips, but sometimes they just bubble up thoughts).
The woman asks her dog to speak, to say a few words
(because perhaps he is just waiting to be asked). But he just looks
at her in that baleful way and goes back to sniffing sidewalk cracks.
If the dog is having a thought, she is not privy to it.

The woman supposes she should assume the fuming,
whimsical pose, with asterisks and exclamation points
hovering over her head. After all, she is in the pitiable
position of talking to an ink-spotted animal on the eve
of the new year while other characters might be wearing
lampshades on their heads or blowing toy kazoos
with champagne fizzing crazily all over the place, the cork
ricocheting off all the walls and dangling chandeliers.
However, this woman will not spare a thought
balloon for such a petty thing. She is glad for the dog,
talking or not, and every exquisitely drawn star of the night.

In a Foreign City

All day I lay in the wreckage
of our bed, the new wound between
my thighs seeping into the sheets.

You'd fled before sallow light stained
the corners of the rented room.
Our bodies' rift seemed another

deep error, after the pressing
together of palms, the plunder
of our kiss. My sleep was so shallow

I woke before each dream's resolution,
wringing the salt-stung scent of you
from the pillow, that flotsam clutched

to my chest. At dusk I rose to look out
the rain-lashed window, knowing
that somewhere in that foreign city,

in your sodden coat, you were still
walking and walking away
from the source of your regret.

IV.

Magnetic Resonance

In the hospital corridor, we hold
my father's films against fluorescent light
to see the soft pearl his brain has shaped
inside itself. We wonder what memory
is the grit around which it has formed,
this tumor that causes a once-sensible
man to slur and lurch, that seizes
his gaze then cuts him loose,
stuttering and stumbling. Somewhere
this shadowy map shows the way

back to his grace, perhaps back
to the winter of my brother's birth
when he is a young man striding
the sidelines, the coach's whistle bouncing
against his chest while dozens
of basketballs gavel the gym floor,
some snicking through the nets.
He calls out to the fast-breaking boys,
a full court press of sneaker squeaks,
knowing he is father to a son, to these

many sons. Or maybe back to his summer
on harvest crew, raking the acres of wheat
behind a combine, singing Buddy Holly
into the heat and dust of South Dakota.
Away from home, he thinks on girls
and chrome-finned cars and not much else,
glad to drink beer with the fellows
after taking the grain to the scales,
to feel that good ache in his arms
from steering wide swaths through the fields.
Or the before-dawn autumn of late boyhood
when he wades scrub brush and corn stubble.

Stepping into the steam of his breath, he hears
the distant cracks of gunfire. A rustling.
He sights and aims. The rifle flinches
against his chest, spent casings lay at his feet.
Back with a brace of pheasants slung over
his shoulder, he enters his mother's kitchen,
the chill and gamy tang still clinging to feathers.
In the basin float the prized gizzards for her.

That boy is this selfsame man who shambles
and conducts other lives in his sleep.
But now in the antiseptic air
of the oncology ward, we trace
the hazy lobes and folds of his brain,
try to locate the place where memory strays,
where he's stowed the earlier hours of today
and disassembled the names of certain trees.
Instead what we read here is grave and vaporous.
This is an invitation to grief.

Hospital Time

Once the door's pneumatic whoosh sucks you in, a sign
shows the way to emergency, oncology, waiting.
Here you'll take instruction in the ways of pain and time.

At the end of any sterile stairwell you will find
grim rooms of crumpled tissues and thumbed-up magazines.
The tepid coffee sippers have sheaves of forms to sign.

They trundle their sick, their injured, while eyeing
the clock channel's second hand sweep of the TV screen,
hours measured in systolic and diastolic time.

On every floor the nurses, efficient and kind,
run the place, keep up the pill cup, helping routine
of pressing fingers to wrist and charting vital signs.

Somewhere wounds are dressed, and through port and line
chemo drips begin little wars in the bloodstream.
Elsewhere someone gets born, a crisis that lasts a lifetime.

Patience. Patience. Time itself is benign.
This is how the body reveals its scheme
of breath and pulse, the persistent design
that instructs you in the ways of pain in time.

Vigil

During this wakeful watching,
how I have become a scholar
of your face, sleep-slackened map
of all that is sovereign in you.
Observing your breath perish
then rise is to witness blood devotion.
A sudden and inexplicable scent
of cedar pervades the room.
Bodies stubbornly persist,
and we want comforting
even when there is none.
If you could but tell it
in your own true tongue,
what a vast indwelling
would be revealed.

Arising

He says he guesses he could get up
and burrow around a bit, so hoists
himself from bed, at last upright
in baggy pajamas. Stooping over
his walker, he makes a question mark
of his body and interrogates the space
before him by shuffle and push.
From deep in the quarry of his chest
he summons the gumption to go.
And so he turtles along, willing himself
to the breakfast table and the plate
of toast that is set there for him.

Ablution

Because one must be naked to get clean,
my dad shrugs out of his pajama shirt,
steps from his boxers and into the tub
as I brace him, whose long illness
has made him shed modesty too.
Seated on the plastic bench, he holds
the soap like a caught fish in his lap,
waiting for me to test the water's heat
on my wrist before turning the nozzle
toward his pale skin. He leans over
to be doused, then hands me the soap
so I might scrub his shoulders and neck,
suds sluicing from spine to buttock cleft.
Like a child he wants a washcloth
to cover his eyes while I lather
a palmful of pearlescent shampoo
into his craniotomy-scarred scalp
and then rinse clear whatever soft hair
is left. Our voices echo in the spray
and steam of this room where once,
long ago, he knelt at the tub's edge
to pour cups of bathwater over my head.
He reminds me to wash behind his ears,
and when he judges himself to be clean,
I turn off the tap. He grips the safety bar,
steadies himself, and stands. Turning to me,
his body is dripping and frail and pink.
And although I am nearly forty,
he has this one last thing to teach me.
I hold open the towel to receive him.

Grand Mal

The aura comes on, and your face,
almost becalmed, dims and strays.
It begins with a twitch, your head
quirking to the side, and then
an electric arc spasms the body
into gnashings and flailings
and thrashings, and she tries
to keep you from falling,
but you do fall, an ugly thud
on the floor, where she kneels
to blunt, as best she can,
your self-punishing fists
and fitful kicks, saying your name.
And from your mouth comes
a primal, torn-open sound,
and like a thunderous day
with little rain, your contortions
begin to quieten and quell,
and at last you lay slack
and insensible with your shoulders
bruised and a bloody tongue.
But mercifully you won't remember
these halting minutes when you go
so deep into yourself it seems to her
you might not, might never, return.

V.

Green Temple

For now, forget the red of tooth and claw—
the great temple and its teachings are green.
Its amplitude is thick and vegetal,
the lobes and clefts of leaves, all cordate,
serrate, and spathe. The leaves that cut
and those that soothe. Such rhythms,
these layerings, they bewilder and teem
in the vaulted corridors of green.

There is gladness in the green-gold tides
of wheat, in the openhandedness of oaks,
and in the river's verdigris creep over
moss-sueded stones, and fishes beneath.
The grass whistle taut between thumbs
brought to the mouth thrums greenly.
Gleaming mallards and teals dabble on ponds,
and among the rushes, dragonfly wings.

Water and sun and soil make green.
Windfall apples and pears, oh yes, pears,
cucumber slice translucence, scalloped
edges of lettuce, glossy-leaved cornstalks,
waxy cabbages, asparagus, okra,
healing tongues of aloe, basil, and beans.
The silo is abandoned, yet vines
still climb its walls with vigor.

In the greeny deeps of the thicket
one finds the fortitude of chlorophyll;

in the winking aurora borealis,
streaks of commonplace joy.
Aphids and thrips move nimbly along
while the jointed mantis devours her mate.
Everything living, everything green, conspires
to thrive and die, every sapling a creed.

Sky Judge

It begins in a certain grassy light,
like something righteously begotten,
the air still and chartreuse and bird-silent.

Rain dimples the dirt while curdling clouds
toil and spin. And then sirens are searing
over town and into the countryside.

Some take heed and head for their cellars.
Others watch the sky and wait until
the downcoming cloud becomes a finger
of God pointing to the plains, reckoning
whole fields of wheat to bow northeast.

The wind's slashings make a savage sound
of conviction, sheared tin and shingles loosed.
The storm harrows the patient acres,
punishing everything to shards, to shreds,

and at last it lifts its tines, grinding on,
moving out. And folks emerge, blinking,
and what they see is straight revelation—

some houses whittled to slivers, others
untouched in the first spears of sunlight.
Like that they are left to search the furrows
and roads, gleaning the chaff of their lives.

In Acadiana

True that it's a moss-hung land of trash and spices,
        a state of drive-thru daiquiri shacks
and of revival trailers promising free Bibles and beans,
        of heart disease and languid French on the radio.
Any dive off the gulf coast highway has Boo Zoo
        on the jukebox and a dozen or so roughnecks
just off the rigs. Each day you've got to wade
        through the warm broth of afternoon.
You've got to learn to live with your own sweat
        and with the sweat of others. Nights
the mosquito truck drives by lackadaisically,
        trailing toxic mist. Folks are kind and canaille.
By this I mean only praise. If this be our poverty,
        then Lord keep us poor, but do keep us.

Hurricane Ike

Unpacking the last boxes from the move,
I fretted the bubble wrap and watched Ike
ginning up in the gulf on the national news,
cataracting the entire screen in a slow whorl.
It was the second storm in as many weeks
and I was wondering just what it was
I had gone and done.
          When the sky got hectic
I dragged the couch cushions into the hall
making a pallet for me and the dog,
whose soft, sorrel coat I nuzzled all night
while the wind stuttered the shutters and whined
at the rag-stuffed sills and rain razored the panes.

In the dullish morning I met my new neighbors
piling oak limbs and soggy whatnot on the curb.
The story was all about the surge, the worst of it,
which was still coming, and sure enough,
it did come, first dousing Cameron, then swelling up
the intracoastal waterway, whelming rice fields
and wetlands and roads.
          It pushed up the Calcasieu
into the lake, crept up coulees and into the town.
From my high porch I watched water lap the piers
of Savoie's house and a couple kayaking down
Sallier Street. Some kids sashayed hip-deep
through backwash, sidestepping flotillas of fire ants.

For weeks after the flood receded there were piles
of warped plywood and mold-mottled drywall.
I alphabetized and shelved my books, bought
an orchid, unrolled the carpets, and settled down.

Pacheco Burn

When summer arrives, it arrives
in fire, and earnestly.

Across the canyon, smoke tinges
the sky to copper and pink,

stenciling pine branches against
this strange solstice light.

From the cabin deck I can hear
the suss of the Pecos.

Ash flakes drift into the open
notebook, onto the dreaming dog.

When at Last I Join

When at last I join the democracy of dirt,
        a tussock earthed over and grass healed,
I'll gladly conspire in my own diminishment.

        Let a pink peony bloom from my chest
and may it be visited by a charm of bees,
        who will then carry the talcum of pollen

and nectar of clover to the grove where they hive.
        Let the honey they make be broken
from its comb, and release from its golden hold,

        onto some animal tongue, my soul.

Spiritus Mundi

Listen around to the long sentence the land is saying,
to the wind rumoring through the aggregate of grasses.

Hear the soft explosions of all that is tilled under,
a scumble of clods cleaved by the blade, the sheared leavings

of wheat, and memory, memory, a root system still
drilling down, searching out moisture, anything that's useful,

anything dear. Do you recognize your own shy gestures
in the weft of the fields? Oh sisters and brothers,

let the gentle tether of our longing keep us here
among the undulant, amber barley and russet oats.

And if all flesh is grass, then let us live humbly, as grasses do.
In sympathy, we shall shiver and bend, pressing our knees

into the earth, turning our faces to the quavering sun.

Other Books in the Crab Orchard Series in Poetry

Muse
Susan Aizenberg

Lizzie Borden in Love:
Poems in Women's Voices
Julianna Baggott

This Country of Mothers
Julianna Baggott

The Black Ocean
Brian Barker

The Sphere of Birds
Ciaran Berry

White Summer
Joelle Biele

Rookery
Traci Brimhall

In Search of the Great Dead
Richard Cecil

Twenty First Century Blues
Richard Cecil

Circle
Victoria Chang

Consolation Miracle
Chad Davidson

The Last Predicta
Chad Davidson

Furious Lullaby
Oliver de la Paz

Names above Houses
Oliver de la Paz

The Star-Spangled Banner
Denise Duhamel

Smith Blue
Camille T. Dungy

Beautiful Trouble
Amy Fleury

Soluble Fish
Mary Jo Firth Gillett

Pelican Tracks
Elton Glaser

Winter Amnesties
Elton Glaser

Strange Land
Todd Hearon

Always Danger
David Hernandez

Heavenly Bodies
Cynthia Huntington

Red Clay Suite
Honorée Fanonne Jeffers